CYRIL AND THE HOUSE OF COMMONS

by Michael Palin

ILLUSTRATED BY CAROLINE HOLDEN

PUFFIN BOOKS

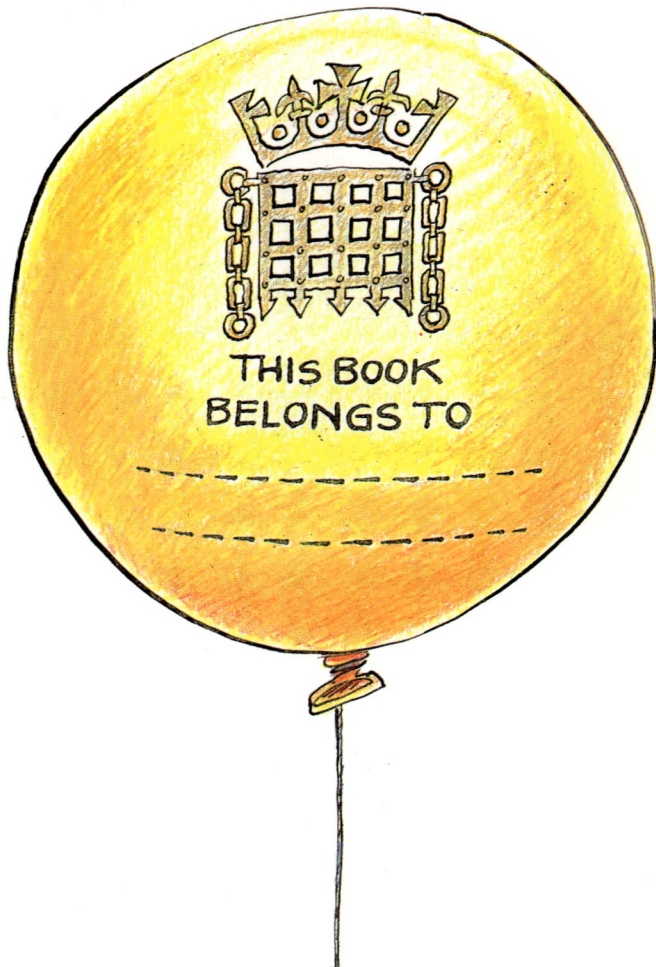

THIS BOOK
BELONGS TO

When Cyril was eight his parents took him to the House of Commons.

Cyril wanted to go to Battersea Funfair, but his mother
said she was tired of taking him to Battersea Funfair, and it
was time he saw how the country was run.

Cyril sat with his parents up in the Public Gallery. A very boring man with a little moustache was talking about reflating the economy. No-one seemed to be listening, in fact most of the Members of Parliament were fast asleep.

Now Cyril was quite an ordinary boy except that he had the power to turn people into other things just by looking at them. Cyril turned his attention to one of the men who was asleep. Within a moment the man (who was the Conservative Member for somewhere near Salisbury) became a large slumbering sheepdog.

A nice lady next to him, who was quite interested in reflating the economy, suddenly noticed him and screamed very loudly.

Everyone stopped and looked at her.
'There's a dog in the House!' she shouted.
By then Cyril had turned the dog back into the
Conservative Member for somewhere near Salisbury so
no-one knew what she was talking about.

'Please would the Honourable Member confine herself to the subject of the debate,' said the Speaker, shortly before he became airborne.

'Good Heavens!' cried the Secretary for Transport, before
he too inflated, broke loose, and drifted across the Chamber.
The two of them made such a pretty picture that Cyril
decided to turn all the Liberals into balloons as well.

As they floated upwards the grim-faced Serjeant-At-Arms, who was supposed to keep order in the House, rushed forward and shouted:

'Don't panic, I'll catch them!'

'Do be careful,' cried the wife of one of the Liberals, who was not at all sure which balloon was her husband.

As the Serjeant-At-Arms rushed forward Cyril turned him into a lovely pool with a fountain, and the two men following him fell in.

The Deputy Speaker decided that, in the event of his superior having become a big red and white striped balloon, he must take charge. So he banged his hammer for order, and all that happened was that a big bell rang behind him.

'Oo, let me have a go!' shouted the Opposition Spokesman on Defence.

'And me! And me!'

Soon most of the Opposition front bench were having a go at banging the hammer and making the bell ring. Meanwhile one of the balloons had burst and showered everyone with sweets and someone had built a waterslide into the pool.

'We should have had one of these in the Commons years ago!' shouted the Member for somewhere near Preston, as he pulled on his trunks and dived in.

The Home Secretary stood up very seriously and wagged his finger:

'This is the sort of behaviour,' but he hadn't got much further before Cyril turned the Home Secretary's finger into a double portion of candy-floss, and he said 'Yippee!' and sat down again, stuffing it into his mouth.

Cyril looked at the Mace, the most august symbol of the authority of Parliament, and as he did so the Mace began to spin, and it came to a halt and pointed to 'Very Kissable' and the Prime Minister went all red.

Somewhere a dog barked and the very boring man with the moustache went on talking about reflating the economy when the Opposition benches began to move, slowly at first, then up and down, gathering speed all the time. Soon they were whizzing round and up and over and down into a watersplash and all the Members screamed and cheered. The noise woke six Government back benchers who had been doing so little that Cyril thought they deserved to be made entirely of wood.

At this the SDP Members, who felt a bit left out, waved their
order papers in the air to attract attention. Cyril felt rather
sorry for them and turned their order papers into coconuts,
which they were soon happily throwing at the back benchers.

'And may I make one further point . . .' went on the man with the little moustache who was still talking about reflating the economy.

The Opposition benches whizzed round ever faster and the Members hung on for dear life as they turned completely upside down and all their pens and wallets fell out of their pockets.

More and more of the Government were jumping in the pool and splashing each other and making a terrible noise. Overhead another of the Liberals burst and toys floated down and the Minister of Agriculture banged the hammer and rang the bell *twice* and won a goldfish.

There was so much noise that Cyril could no longer hear the very boring man with the moustache talking about reflating the economy. Cyril had become very interested in reflating the economy by this time, so he turned everyone else back to normal so he could listen.

But no sooner had he done so than his father gave a big
yawn.

'I'm bored with all this,' he said.

'Me too' said Cyril's mother.

So despite Cyril's protests they took him to Battersea
Funfair after all.